# What To Name Your Jewish Baby

BOOKS BY BILL ADLER

*The Kennedy Wit*
*The Churchill Wit*
*The Stevenson Wit*
*The Johnson Humor*
*Kids' Letters to President Kennedy*
*Dear President Johnson*
*Love Letters to the Mets*
*Love Letters to the Beatles*
*Letters from Camp*
*John F. Kennedy and the Young People of America*
*Boys Are Very Funny People*

# *What To Name* YOUR JEWISH BABY

**by Bill Adler with Arnie Kogen**

**Illustrations by Mort Drucker**

*New York  /  E. P. Dutton & Co., Inc.  /  1966*

Published simultaneously in Canada by Clarke, Irwin & Company Limited, Toronto and Vancouver

Library of Congress Catalog Card Number: 66–11549

The authors wish to express appreciation to Paul Laiken for his assistance in preparing this book

# What To Name Your Jewish Baby

Years ago, all Jewish children were named Sol or Irving. Then came the Sheldons, Melvins and Arnolds. Now they're all named Mitchell, Keith and Scott. We knew a couple who recently had the courage to name their child "Murray." Today a name like that can be embarrassing — especially when the little girl grows up.

This book is humbly and respectfully dedicated to all those doting Jewish parents who want to give their offspring a name with class, sex appeal, urbanity, distinction, and mainly one that will look good on a camp name tape.

At last, the creative Jewish parents can do more than just name their baby after a grandparent, sister-in-law, distant cousin or pick a name out of a hat. (We don't even want to discuss how many kids have been named "Stetson" via this method). Now every Jewish baby can have a name with substance and elegance and meaning.

Remember, it was once said by a great philosopher: "He who steals my money steals trash. But he who steals my name steals *Gold*!" This was said by Harvey Gold. (Brooklyn Small Claims Court. Case #LXVII. Jan. 23, 1935. 'Gold vs. the City of N.Y.')

We agree with Harvey. Read through this book. You'll agree with him also.

Bill Adler

Arnie Kogen

# GIRLS

**ABBY** — Hebrew: Abigayil. *My Father is joy.*
  "Dear Abby" — gossip columnist.

Abby will undoubtedly grow up to be her school Yenta. She will be the first lady in her apartment building to take a bridge chair out in front and sit there. This will cause quite a commotion, since the building is still under construction.

**ADELPHA** — Greek: Adelph. *Sisterly.*

Adelpha is gonna have one helluva problem finding a husband.

**ADRIENNE** — Latin: Adria, Hadria. *Dark one.*

Adrienne will be thrown out of the lounge at the Concord Hotel — for starting a Conga line. The next morning she will begin cha-cha lessons at the cabana — and be thrown into the pool!

**AGATHA** — Greek: Agathe. *Good, kind.*
Agatha Christie — noted English novelist.

Agatha Birnbaum, noted eighteenth-century American — Jewish novelist. Famous for writing with a quill dipped in chicken fat. Her most celebrated book, *The Wandering Jew Comes Home for Yom Kippur.*

**AGNES** — Greek: Hagne. *Pure one.*

The goddess Agnes, like a polished diamond, reflected all the colors of the spectrum. The Jewish Agnes will be the only girl in her nursery school to blush the color of borscht.

**ALERIA** — Middle Latin: Alarie. *Eaglelike.*

Aleria will undoubtedly have a nose job by the time she's a sophomore in high school.

**ALLISON** — Irish Gaelic. *Little truthful one.*
Allison MacKenzie, character on TV soap opera.

Allison will grow up in the Jewish Peyton Place — Great Neck, Long Island.

**AMABEL** — Latin: Amabilis. *Sweet, soft, and beautiful.*

Amabel is lovely, she's engaged, she uses Brillo with kosher soap pads.

**AMY** — French: Aimee. *Beloved.*
Amy Lowell, American poet, Pulitzer Prize winner (1874–1925).

Amy Levitsky, beloved Bronx poetess (Public School 209) received a standing ovation in assembly, when she recited her famous work: "Twinkle, twinkle, little star, are you made of Halvah?"

**ANDREA** — Latin: Andrea. *Womanly.*

Andrea will go to the beauty parlor twice a week to have her hair "frosted." She will sleep standing up and won't let her husband near her.

**APRIL** — Latin: Aprilis. *Opening; blooming.*

April will have a shower when she's engaged. It will be a typical surprise shower. When she comes in, she'll be so shocked — that she'll drop her thank-you cards.

**ARABELLA** — Latin: Ara-bella. *Beautiful altar.*

If she plays her cards right, this girl will be standing on one with a chupa over it, by the time she's twenty. She will have to — for the baby's sake.

**ARLENE** — Irish Gaelic: Airleas. *A pledge.*
Arlene Francis, TV panelist on "What's My Line?"

Your Jewish Arlene will grow up to be a TV personality. She will be guest panelist on "What's My Line?" and will guess the occupations of those in wholesale only. She will also make appearances on the "Ed Solomon Show," "Gunshmoe," "Batman and Flanken," "My Tanta, the Car," "The Eleven o'Clock — Maybe a Few Minutes After Eleven — News," "The Most Mishugana Ship in the Army," and "The Wide World of Schwartz."

**ASTA** — Greek: Aster. *Star; starlike.*

Asta was a Greek goddess who imbued men with high resolutions. She was also Jewish, and one of the resolutions she told her own son was, "Look, Herbie, there are a lot of refined girls here in Greece. And believe me, it's just as easy to marry a rich one as a poor one." Asta went on to become famous. Herbie never got married.

**ASTRID** — Old Norse: As-tryd. *Divine strength.*

Astrid will grow up to be a *schtarkah*. She will work summers as athletic director at a hotel in the mountains. When she leaves, the guests will chip in and buy her a truss.

**AUDREY** — Old English: Aethelthryth. *Noble strength; strength to overcome life's difficulties.*

Audrey will have the strength to overcome all of life's difficulties. She will only crack up on the day her son comes into her Scarsdale home and announces that he wants to marry a girl from East Flatbush.

**BATHSHEBA** — Hebrew: Bathsheba. *Daughter of the oath; seventh daughter.*

Bathsheba is your seventh daughter. She will never take a bath because she will never be able to get into the bathroom.

**BEATRICE** — Latin: Beatrix. *She who makes others happy.*

Beatrice will make her husband happy. She will be a Jewish nymphomaniac. A Jewish nymphomaniac is one who lets her husband make love to her after she comes back from the beauty parlor.

**BENEDICTA** — Latin: Benedicta. *Blessed one.*

People will keep shouting "Gesundheit!" at Benedicta. Better get her a large box of Kleenex and a good nose spray.

**BERNADETTE** — French: Bernard-ette. *Brave as a bear.*

Bernadette will claw her way to a career as an assistant buyer in a half-size house.

**BERNICE** — Greek: Berenkie. *Bringer of victory.*

Bernice will bring ultimate victory to her family. She will be one of those girls who will wait until she's married to have expensive dental work done and have her nose fixed. She figures, "Let her new husband pay the bills; why burden the family?"

**BERTHA** — Old German: Perahta. *Shining; glorious one.*
   The original Bertha was the old German fertility goddess.

This girl's only hope is to fall in love with an obstetrician.

**BLANCHE** — Old French: Blanch. *White or blonde; Fair one.*

Blanche will be the first on her block to bleach her hair. Only her hairdresser will know for sure. Then she will tell her girl friend Muriel, and everybody in the neighborhood will know. Only her hairdresser will not find out about this.

**BONNIE** — Middle English: Bonie. *Good one.*

Bonnie is the typical good girl. Brought up by very strict, Orthodox parents, she is the type that says, "Please, not here." She says this to her husband on their honeymoon.

**BRENDA** — Old English: Brand. *Firebrand.*

Brenda Berkowitz, famous Jewish call girl. Did so well she had an unlisted answering service number.

**BRUNHILDA** — Old German: Bruni-hilde. *Armored warrior maiden.*

Brunhilda will be a Zoftic girl from the age of three. She will require a corset at her Bas Mitzvah. It will be one of those girdles that let you breathe. Unfortunately this girdle will have asthma — and Brunhilda will explode during the ceremony.

**CANDACE (CANDY)** — Greek: Kandake. *Glittering; glowing white.*

Her half of the class in Hebrew school had 22 percent fewer cavities. Because her half of the class had 48 percent more boys studying to be dentists.

**CAROL** — Latin: Carola. *Strong and womanly.*
  Carol Heiss, famous American figure skater.

Carol Horowitz, famed Israeli figure skater. During the national finals in Haifa she went crazy trying to make a figure אּ.

**CAROLINE** — Latin-French: Caroline. *Little, womanly one.*

Caroline will mature and become a little woman very quickly. At the age of 13 her mother will buy her a Living Bra, but it will die of malnutrition.

**CATHERINE** — Greek: Katharos. *Pure one.*

To Catherine her mother will warn: "Go, go — have a nice vacation in the mountains. But if you come home with even *one* pimple missing, I'll murder you!" Catherine's acne clears up the first night there.


**CHINA** — Oriental: Asiatic country.

China will be half-Oriental — half-Jewish. She will be an *"Orieyenta."*


**CHLOE** — Greek: Chloe. *Young verdant.*

A great name to give your girl if you happen to live in a swamp.


**CHRISTINE** — French: Christine. *Christian.*

Not a Jewish name for a girl. If it's a boy and you happen to live in Denmark — OK.


**CLARA** — Latin: Clara. *Brilliant; bright; illustrious.*

It was a Clara who got up in the middle of a packed dining room at Grossinger's and shouted hysterically: "Is there a doctor in the house?" "Is there a doctor in the house?!" Four young men rushed over to her and said, "We're doctors, What is it?" She pointed to the shy young lady next to her and said, "Gentlemen — I'd like you to meet my daughter — Muriel."


**CLAUDIA** — Latin: Claudia. *Delicate; modest.*

Claudia will be so modest that she won't let her husband look at her in the nude. She will not realize, however, that he once saw her in the nude and doesn't care anymore.

**CLEOPATRA** — Greek: Cleopatra. *Father's glory or fame.*

What's a nice Egyptian girl like her doing in a book like this? We recommend a different name for your Jewish baby. If however you do insist on calling her Cleopatra, we suggest you immediately take her to your pediatrician for diptheria, smallpox and asp shots.

**CORA** — Greek: Kore. *The maiden.*

Cora will be a servant — she will wait hand and foot on the thing she loves most — her Wednesday night Mah-Jongg group. Her husband will be left to make his own supper.

**CYNTHIA** — Greek: Kynthia. *Moon goddess.*

Any kid named Cynthia will be an "also" girl and never have her own identity. When you invite the family to dinner, you'll say, "Oh, yes, and bring Cynthia also." Because of overcrowded preschool conditions, Cynthia will be forced to attend "night nursery." She will be the only child in the neighborhood to participate in flag lowering and salute dusk.

**DAGMAR** — Old German: Dagomar. *Famous thinker.*
   Dagmar — TV star, early 1950's.

If you name your daughter Dagmar she undoubtedly will have something to do with the Community Chest.

**DEBORAH** — Hebrew: Deborah. *The bee; industrious.*

Girls named Deborah are the types who are so industrious that they clean the house *before* the girl shows up on Thursday. It was a Deborah Teittlebaum who was so neat that her husband got up in the middle of the night to get a glass of water — and when he came back, his bed was made.

**DELMA** — French: Delmare. *Of the sea.*

Delma is the girl who goes to a resort and always ends up being given mouth-to-mouth resuscitation by the lifeguard. Strangely enough, Delma never goes swimming.

**DINAH** — Hebrew: Dinah. *Judged.*
   In the Bible, Dinah was the daughter of Jacob and Leah.

She was also an eighth cousin to King David on Leah's side, and a fifth cousin to Samuel from Jacob's family; besides being the aunt of Moses by Leah's second cousin. She was also distantly related to Lot — and had a secret crush on Mordecai whom she first met at Haman's hanging. With this kind of background, Dinah is sure to be a force at family functions and Cousins Club meetings. At these meetings, Dinah brings up the subject of burial plots.

**DIANA** — Latin: Diana. *Goddess of the hunt.*

Diana will go to every Singles Weekend at the Concord Hotel until she is 47. She usually ends up the weekend by asking the fellow: "Is this just a summer thing, or will you call me in the city?" In her 47 years, *no one* has ever called Diana in the city.

**DORENE** — Irish Gaelic: Doire-ann. *The sullen one.*

Dorene is always complaining — always arguing with her husband. She always ends each argument by shouting, "You're gonna drive me to my grave!" In two minutes, he has the car in front of the door.

**DORIS** — Greek: Doris. *From the ocean.*

Doris will buy a $145 bathing suit, an $80 bathing cap, ermine water wings — and then spend the day sitting under a beach umbrella, thinking of ways *not* to go in the ocean. The rule is: Jewish girls *never* get their hair wet. At most, they'll step into the water, hang onto a rope — and dunk themselves.

**EDITH** — Old English: Eadgyth. *Rich gift.*

Every family should have an Edith. She is always good for at least a $75 gift bond at every Bar Mitzvah, wedding or briss. No one can figure out how she an afford it — on the $1,500 insurance her husband left her.

**EDNA** — Hebrew: 'ednah. *Rejuvenation.*

Hurricanes are usually named Edna which has nothing to do with *What to Name Your Jewish Baby,* but is important for our next volume, *What to Name Your Jewish Hurricane.*

**ELEANOR** — Old French: Elienor. *Light.*

Eleanor is the one who usually lights up the conversation with philosophical gems such as, "You should live and be well," "A son I got, he should only bust," and the brilliant, "When you're in the neighborhood, don't be a stranger." No one will ever visit Eleanor.

**ELIZABETH** — British; Consecrated to God. Yiddish: Elizabeaut. *The pussycat.*
    Elizabeth Taylor — American, English, Jewish actress. Screen siren.

Elizabeth Trubowitz, famous siren of Mosholu Parkway, the Bronx. Had 63 affairs by the time she was 18. All of them were catered. When asked if she believed in premarital sex relations, she replied, "Not if it delays the ceremony."

**ELLA** — Old English. Aelf. *Beautiful fairy maiden.*

Ella usually winds up living in Greenwich Village with another girl. But don't worry, the other girl is always Jewish.

**ELLIE** — Greek: Elias. *Jehovah is God.*

Ellie is the schoolteacher who goes to Europe every year on her summer vacation. Plump Ellie Epplebaum of Atlantic City — went to Rome last summer, and while walking along the Via Veneto, slapped eight Italian men! Not one of them would pinch her.

**EMILY** — Gothic: Amala. *Industrious one.*

Emily will do anything to get a husband. One Emily we know was so shocked when her boy friend Harvey proposed to her — that she nearly fell off the bed.

**ESTELLE** — French: Estile. *A star.*

Estelle is cut out to be an actress. Because wherever her husband takes her — restaurants, theater, parties — or Cousins Club meetings — she ends up making a scene.

**ESTHER** — Hebrew: Esthur. *A star.*

Queen Esther of Persia was very extravagant. She was the only queen in history ever to lay carpeting across the entire country. What's worse, she made everybody take off his shoes.

**FELICE** — Latin: Felicia. *Happy one.*

Felice is very happy and will have a great sense of humor. She will laugh at everything her husband does. That's why they will never have children.

**FENELLA** — Irish Gaelic: Fionnghuala. *White-shouldered one.*

Fenella will have a dandruff problem. For a practical present now, we suggest you get her a gift certificate to Wig City.

**FLORA** — Latin: Flora. *Flower.*

Flora will live in suburbia. She will force her husband Milton to keep up with the Joneses. She will insist on having a phone in the car — but will complain when she has to keep running out to the garage to answer it.

**FLORENCE** — Latin: Florentia. *Blooming; flourishing; prosperous.*

Florence usually marries well — and is always the first in her circle to go to Europe. It was a Florence who was bragging to her friends about her trip to Rome. "And did you see the Pope?" one of them asked. "Are you kidding? I *dined* with him," she exaggerated. "What did you think of him?" "Well," she replied, "he was wonderful — but his wife I didn't care for."

**FRIEDA** — Old German: Fridu. *Peaceful one.*

Frieda is very peaceful but also very naïve. She thinks sex is a store on Fifth Avenue.

**GAY** — Old French: Gai. *Bright and lively.*

If she's so bright, let her make up her own joke about her name.

**GEORGIA** — Latin: Georgia. *Farmer.*

A Southern girl, Georgia sings "I wish I was in the land of cotton." Her wish comes true when she ends up working as a receptionist* in New York's garment center.

*The more zoftik Georgias will also work in the garment center — as shipping clerks.

**GINA** — Latin: Segina. *A queen.*

Gina will be treated like a queen and will be spoiled. It was Gina Lola Berkowitz of East End Avenue who at the age of nine said indignantly to her parents, "I'm running away from home — call me a cab."

**GOLDIE** — Old English: Goldie. *Golden one.*

Will have beautiful blonde hair at the age of seven — but her *roots* will be black. When she's married she will ask her husband, "Morris, will you love me when I'm old and gray?" "Why not — I've loved you through every other color."

**HANNAH** — Hebrew: Khannah. *Graceful one.*

This girl will become a famous dance instructor. Hannah will eventually open up a swinging discothèque in Tel Aviv. It will be called Let My People A Go Go.

**HARRIET** — Old French: Hanriette. *Estate or home ruler.*

If you're married to a Harriet — forget it! She rules the house with an iron hand. A nut on neatness, she won't let you use the bathroom towels. "Don't touch them, it's for the company!" So — after you take a shower, you stand there like an idiot — drying yourself with toilet paper. Harriet is the type who buys $20,000 worth of living room furniture and then doesn't let anyone into the living room. Everyone has to congregate in the *foyer.* One Harriet we know (Harriet Blechman, of Scarsdale), went so far as to buy new furniture, but she was afraid someone would scratch it . . . so she kept it in storage for three years.

**HAZEL** — Old English: Haesel. *Hazelnut tree.*

Hazel is a Jewish nut. On a test in Hebrew school, she thought Yom Kippur was a Japanese admiral. When she grows up, Hazel becomes a nurse. She is the one who made history at Beth Israel Hospital when she suggested that they take the patient with a 104-degree temperature and put him in bed with a man with the chills — to level him off.

**HEDDA** — Old German: Hadu. *Strife.*

Hedda will give her husband nothing but strife. She will start an argument right after the wedding. Lawyers will be brought in to see who gets custody of the wedding cake.

**HELEN** — Greek: Helene. *Light; a torch.*

Helen will constantly be carrying a torch . . . or a flashlight. She will end up being an usherette in a Yiddish theater on Second Avenue.

**HILDA** — Old German: Hilde. *Battle maid.*

Hilda will spend her life battling with maids. Some won't do ironing, others won't do heavy cleaning, and nobody wants to do the windows. Hilda is the type who draws a line around the liquor bottle to see if anybody drank from it while she was away.

**IDA** — Old English: Eada. *Prosperous; happy.*

Did you ever see a Jewish girl that was happy without being prosperous also? Ida will become prosperous by marrying a gypsy. They will have a chain of empty stores.

**IMOGENE** — Latin: Imaginis. *An image or likeness.*

Imogene is a small image of her mother. Her father will hate her on sight.

**INGRID** — Old Norse: Ing-rida. *Here's a daughter.*
  Ingrid Bergman — actress.

Ingrid is not a name for a Jewish girl. Bergman is.


**IRENE** — Greek: Eirene. *Peace.*

Irene is the family peacemaker. In any argument involving wedding invitations — such as "who should be invited," "which cousins *shouldn't* be invited," "who will be insulted if they're *not* invited," and the ever popular, "who should sit at the table with
Aunt Frieda?" — Irene will be consulted. She won't be *invited,*
but she'll be consulted.


**IRIS** — Greek: Iris. *The rainbow.*

Iris believes there's a pot of gold at the end of the rainbow. She
ends up marrying a man named Gold — with a pot.


**ISABEL** — Old Spanish: Ysabel. *Consecrated to God.*
  Isabel (Isabella), Queen of Spain, gave Columbus money to sail
  to America.

Unknown to history Isabel of Israel in the fifteenth century also
commissioned three Jewish ships — The *Moishe,* The *Pippick,*
and the *Shleppe Maria* — to discover a short route to the new
world. This was the only fleet of ships with a social director. They
took 12 years to make the trip. They would have done it sooner,
but they stopped off at the Virgin Islands to go shopping.


**IVY** — Old English: Ifig. *Ivy vine.*

Ivy will go to an exclusive girls' school like Vassar, Smith, Bryn
Mawr or Yeshiva on the Hudson. She will be a wild, uninhibited,
eccentric nonconformist. Everything she does will be different.
She will spend her childhood living with her parents in Greenwich
Village. Then, at the age of 22 she will move out and get an apart-
ment of her own in Forest Hills.

**JANE** — Hebrew: Y-hohhanan. *Graciousness.*

Jane is the type who's very gracious with her fiancé when figuring out the wedding invitations. It ends up with 200 people invited — 199 from her side. He has his choice of his father or mother.

**JESSICA** — Hebrew: Yishay. *Wealthy one.*

Jessica will constantly be spoiled by her wealthy parents. She'll be the only girl on Long Island with a rhinestone skateboard. At the age of eight, her chauffeured limousine will stop in front of a Miami hotel. Her father will get out and order two bellhops to carry her into the hotel. A lady will walk by and say, "Can't she walk?" Her father will look at the lady and say, "Thank God, she doesn't have to!"

**JOAN** — Hebrew: Y-hohhanan. *God is gracious.*
Joan of Arc — French heroine — accused of witchcraft.

Joan will be very superstitious. She will refuse to cook in any week that has a Friday in it.

**JOSEPHINE** — Hebrew: Yoseph. *He shall add.*

This girl has got to wind up being married to a CPA.

**JOY** — Latin: Joia. *Joyful one; gladness.*
She was like a girl enchanted, enraptured by all life.

Joys are always happy when shopping for bargains. Joy Mendelson, of Coney Island, found a fantastic bargain last year when she discovered an appetizing store that was having a January White Fish Sale.

**JUDITH** — Hebrew: Yehudith. *Praised.*
A woman commended for her patience and womanliness.

Judith Fineberg was just such a woman of patience. On a vacation weekend in 1953, she sat at the same table with a young MD — and had the patience to wait until the appetizer was served before mentioning her daughter Sylvia.

**JULIA** — Latin: Julia. *Youthful one.*

Julia Jacobson, famous Jewish hussy. She was desired by men from Rockaway to Westchester because she kept her youthful figure. The figure was $80,000 left to her when she was 13 by her Uncle Abe from Philadelphia.

**KAREN** — Greek: Kore. *The maiden.*

Karen is an old-fashioned Jewish girl. At dances, she still dips. She won't let anybody kiss her until the second date. Trouble is, Karen never has a second date.

**KEELY** — Irish Gaelic: Cadhla. *Beautiful one.*

Keely Markowitz, first girl ever to pose for a foldout in the B'nai B'rith Newsletter, 1949. She was voted Miss Tvilim by the United Rabbis of America, 1950.


**KIM** — Old English: Cyne. *Chief; ruler.*
  Kim Novak — actress.

Kim Ahere, famed Yiddish actress in the same tradition as her American namesakes. Kim's latest pictures, *Mohel Flanders* and *Of Human Bandage* are playing art theaters on Delancey Street.


**LANA** — Irish Gaelic: Alain. *Bright; fair; beautiful.*
  Lana Turner, movie actress (discovered sitting on a stool, Schwab's Drugstore, Hollywood).

Lana Liebowitz, garment center receptionist. Spent an afternoon sitting on a stool at Ratner's Dairy Restaurant, Second Avenue. Not only wasn't she discovered, but she was fired for taking too long a lunch hour. She then went on and crashed the movies — Loew's Pitkin in Brooklyn.


**LAURA** — Latin: Laurea. *A crown of laurel leaves.*

Laura won't be much for laurel leaves but she'll be a fanatic about planting trees in Israel.


**LEAH** — Hebrew: Leah. *Weary one.*

Leah is typical of the millions of weary upper-middle-class Jewish housewives. She'll spend a whole day slaving over a hot take-out menu.


**LENA** — Latin: Lena. *She who allures.*

Lena will be a party girl. Hired to entertain men at stag parties. Unfortunately she will be allergic to whipped cream cakes — and at Herbie Zimmerman's bachelor party, she will startle everyone by jumping naked out of a giant cheese Danish.

**LILLIAN** — Latin: Lilium. *A lily flower.*

Lillians are usually proud grandmothers. They are not old enough to be *bubbas*. *Bubbas* are over 65. Lillians are always 45-60, still wear stretch slacks, and usually have the gray in their hair frosted blonde. As soon as they meet you, Lillians immediately show you pictures of their grandchildren. Most just show wallet photos — but some *really* proud Lillians carry movie projectors with them.

**LINDA** — Spanish: Linda. *Pretty one.*

Lindas are very pretty, but they are known for giving their husbands a rough time. Lindas are the ones who insist on sleeping in a dual bed — so that when their husbands come near them in the middle of the night they can roll away on their half of the bed.

**LOLA** — Spanish: Dolores. *Sorrows.*

Remember, whatever Lola wants — Lola gets. In fact it was Lola Flamowitz who wanted a mink coat so badly that when she finally got it — she was in no condition to button it.

**LOUISE** — Old German: Hlutwig. *Famous in battle.*

Louise is the type who will always argue with her husband. She will want an ermine coat and he will want a new car. They will compromise. Louise will get an ermine coat and they will keep it in the garage.

**LUCY** — Latin: Lucia. *Light; bringer of light.*

Lucy will probably end up working in a beauty parlor in Scarsdale — in charge of the bleach department.

**MABEL** — Latin: Amabilis. *Lovable one.*

All the boys in the neighborhood will love and adore Mabel. They will worship the ground her father struck oil on.

**MADELINE** — Greek: Magdaline. *Elevated; magnificent; tower of strength.*

To the Madelines of this world, the term a "tower of strength" means a luxury apartment with a terrace in a rent-controlled building.

**MARCIA** — Latin: Marcia. *Belonging to Mars; martial one.*

Marcia's husband will be the first Jewish astronaut to travel to Mars. Her final words to him on the launching pad will be: "Listen, Murray — the trip takes two months. So to let me know you arrived safely — the *minute* you land, give me one ring and ask for yourself!"

**MARGARET** — Latin: Margarita. *A pearl.*
   Margaret Mead — anthropologist.

Margaret "Maivan" Moskowitz, anthropology major at Brooklyn College. Famous for taking a group of Hillel students on a tour of Africa. The trip was immensely successful. None of them made important findings, but all the girls ended up marrying witch doctors.

**MARILYN** — Hebrew: Marah. *Bitter or bitterness.*

Marilyns have reason to be bitter. They are always being disappointed. One Marilyn came home after an afternoon Mah-Jongg game and found her husband in the arms of her maid. She was hysterical for weeks after. Her mother tried to console her. "Don't worry, dear, you can always find another husband." She said, "Husband, who cares? I miss the *maid!*"

**MARJORIE** — Old French: Margerie. *A pearl.*

If your daughter is named Marjorie, she is destined to follow in the footsteps of the famous Jewish heroine, Marjorie Morningstar. She will move from the Bronx to West End Avenue — to Central Park West — to Central Park South — to Scarsdale — where she will then meet all her old girl friends from the Bronx. Name your kid Marjorie only if you already live in Scarsdale.

**MARTHA** — Aramaic: Martha. *Lady or mistress.*

Martha Bernstein, mistress of the most beautiful home in Forest Hills. She was a gracious hostess. When her father-in-law visited for a weekend, she said: "Poppa, I want you to feel as though our home is your home." He did. The next day he sold it.

**MATHILDA** — Old German: Mat-hilde. *Mighty battle maiden.*

You will hear little of Mathilda when she grows up. She will be drafted into the Israeli Army.

**MAXINE** — Latin: Maxima. *Greatest.*

Maxine will be the greatest daughter-in-law in the world. She will keep a kosher home just to please her in-laws. She will be so Orthodox that she won't allow the kids to bring a piggy bank into the house.

**MILDRED** — Old English: Mildraed. *Mild counselor.*

Mildred will become a counselor at one of the famous camps: Camp Cherokee, Camp Sequoia or Camp Tuscarora. Then, later on she will open up her *own* camp — called "Camp Berkowitz." This will be the first Jewish camp — attended by *Indian children.*

**MIMI** — Hebrew: Miryam. *Bitter.*

Mimi will take out her bitterness by having a succession of affairs. She will also have no respect for her husband. Mimi will order towels from Bloomingdales marked Hers and Shleps. One day her husband will come home and find her in the arms of another man. He will shout, "What do you think you're doing?" Mimi will turn to her lover and say, "See, I told you he was stupid."

**MINNIE** — Old German: Minne. *Beloved; resolute protector.*

Minnies are always kindly old grandmothers who try to cure you when you get a cold. They always have their own special remedies. "Drink a cup of hot tea, a little chicken soup, put it all in a sock, face the east, and throw some salt over your shoulder." Surprisingly enough, it always works!

**MOLLY** — Hebrew: Marah. *Bittersweet.*
Molly Picon, actress. "Molly Goldberg"

Mollies almost always turn out to be *bubbas* and grandmothers.
They are lovable, affectionate and are always called in to baby-sit.
("The kids are anxious to see you, Ma — besides, we couldn't get
our regular sitter.") Molly epitomizes the definition of a Jewish
grandmother: "An old lady who sits by the fire and keeps your
mother from hitting you."

**NANCY** — Hebrew: Hannah. *Graceful one.*
   A magic name for beauty walking.

Nancy will start shaving her legs by the time she's 15. At 25 nature will fight back and she will have a moustache.

**NAOMI** — Hebrew: Naomi. *The pleasant one.*

Naomi is the good sport in the family. She's the one who always has the Family Circle meeting in *her* house. After cooking a meal, serving them coffee and cake, watching them throw their coats on her bed (nearly suffocating her two kids who are sleeping there), she ends up doing the dishes by herself. The whole family loves Naomi, but she never gets invited to any of *their* homes.

**NARDA** — Latin: Nardus. *Fragrant ointment.*

Narda is the girl who puts on loads of skin cream, face cream and ointment before she goes to bed at night. When her husband goes to kiss her — she slides out of his arms.

**NATALIE** — Latin: Natalis. *Birthday or natal day.*

From the day she's born, Natalie will kvetch a lot. They are born complainers. Natalie Nusselbaum, inventor of famous phrases of Jewish mothers — among them, "Will you please do something about *your* son." "Go bring up children!" "Wait till you have children of your own someday." And the ever popular, "This is the thanks I get?"

**NEVA** — Spanish: Nieve. *Snow or extreme whiteness.*

*Neva on Sunday.* Like all other modern Jewish girls, Neva will refuse on Sundays to do the one thing her husband wants — cook! He will end up taking her out for Chinese food.

**NICOLE** — Greek: Nikolaos. *Victorious army; victorious people.*

Nicole Margolis, first Playboy bunny in Israel. Had to leave when she couldn't pass her rabbit test.

**NORMA** — Latin: Norma. *A lady of perfection.*

Norma Dubinsky, famous Jewish lady of perfection. Living on Central Park South, she had to have everything "just so." She wanted to get rid of her husband, Morris, because he clashed with the drapes.

**ODELIA** — Old Anglo-French: Odel. *Little wealthy one.*

Odelia Offenberg — the only girl in PS 238 to come to school wearing a Captain Marvel Decoder ring — in a Tiffany setting. At the age of five, Odelia's father bought her some blocks to play with — Flatbush Avenue, Riverside Drive and Tremont Avenue.

**ODESSA** — Greek: Odysseia. *The odyssey; a long journey.*

Odessa will go far. Let her.

**OLGA** — Old Norse: Halog. *Holy one.*

Olga is usually a Jewish girl living in the North Woods. The only way this girl will get a mink is by trapping one.

**OLIVIA** — Latin: Olivia. *Olive tree or olive branch.*
  The olive branch is symbolic of peace.

Our Olivia will be quiet and peaceful. She is the type of a girl who will hold hands with her husband Bernie all the time. This is because if they ever let go, she'll kill him!

**OPAL** — Sanskrit: Upala. *A precious stone.*

Opal is the girl in the neighborhood who walks around with the biggest and most expensive jewelry. For diamonds and rubies she'll do anything. One evening at a party another lady was admiring her ring — a beautiful 37-carat sparkler. The lady was amazed. She inquired, "What is it? I've never seen one like that." Opal said, "It's the Klopstone Diamond; it's the most valuable diamond in the hemisphere, but it comes with a curse." The lady inquired, "What's the curse?" Opal pointed to a balding, aged old man at the bar. *"Mr.* Klopstone."

**PAMELA** — Greek: Pam-meli. *All-honey.*

As a child, Pamela is the one who will bring the honey cake to her grandmother's house for Passover. When she grows up, she will be an outstanding cook and will excel in cooking the two favorite Jewish foods of all time — chow mein and pizza.

**PATIENCE** — French: Patience. *Endurance with fortitude.*

Patience will have plenty to endure. She will have four children and live in 2½ rooms in the West Bronx. It was Patience who was the first to say, "Children should be seen and not had."

**PATRICIA** — Latin: Patricius. *Noble one; high born.*

Patricia Horowitz, wealthiest child ever to be born in Brooklyn Jewish Hospital. She was born with a silver ladle in her mouth. She was the only newborn in history to tip the doctor upon arrival.

**PAULINE** — Latin: Paulus. *Little.*
Small in stature but big in love and constancy.

Pauline Plotkin is the world's smallest Jewish lady. She has a job weekends for a Bronx catering hall — standing on wedding cakes.


**POMONA** — Latin: Pomona. *Fruitful; motherhood.*

Better take out Blue Cross, and reserve *now* for a semiprivate at Mount Sinai.


**RACHEL** — Hebrew: Rachel. *A ewe.*
The biblical Rachel was a personification of gentleness and patience while suffering.

Rachels usually have problems. Most Rachels have an obsession with neatness. Rachel Rabinowitz, of Bayside, visited a psychiatrist — she spent the first hour rearranging the location of his couch.


**RAMONA** — Spanish: Ramona. *Mighty or wise protector.*

Ramona Rothchild, while putting her son Herbie to bed, said, "Now close your eyes and go to sleep because the sandman is coming." Herbie said, "Give me a dollar and I won't tell Daddy."


**ROBERTA** — Old English: Hroth-Beorht. *Shining with fame.*
Roberta Peters — opera star.

Gentile Robertas usually wind up opera stars. However, when most Jewish Robertas are asked whether they are interested in the Metropolitan, they usually say, "Maybe; how big is the policy?"

**ROCHELLE** — French: Rochelle. *From the little rock.*

Rochelle Glassman — famous Yiddish secretary. From her we got the name of that famous Westchester city. As a girl, Rochelle went to the mountains for the weekend — to look for a husband. When she came home, her mother took her aside and inquired, *"Nu, Rochelle?"*

**ROSE** — Greek: Rhodos. *A rose.*

Rose is always the lady in the flowered hat who's in charge of theater parties for her organization. She has never had too much success. She was the one who arranged for tickets to *Kelly* — and before that three shows that closed in Philadelphia.

**ROXANNE** — Persian: Raokhsha. *Brilliant one.*

Roxanne Schwartz, a night school prodigy at C.C.N.Y., 1951-55. Majored in Cooking, excelled in Intermediate Kasha. Famous for her term paper, "101 Ways to Pickle a Lox."

**RUBY** — Old French: Rubi. *A jewel.*

Jewels will play a very important part in every Ruby's life. One Ruby we heard about was married to a man who had wealth, but was very stingy. She became very ill and just before she died she commissioned an artist to paint her portrait, and around her neck she had him paint an expensive diamond necklace — in addition to four diamond rings glittering from her fingers. Her friend asked her, "Ruby, why did you have the painter paint in all that jewelry?" She said, "Because after I die, and my husband remarries, I want to drive that second wife crazy — looking around the house, trying to find out where I kept it."

**SALLY** — Tin Pan Alley: Sally. *Missing one.*

Name the kid this and you'll wonder what became of her.

**SARAH** — Hebrew: Sarah. *Princess.*

Sarah was the first Jewish wife. She was married to Abraham who was the first Jewish husband. Sarah got Abraham crazy, looking around for a nice Jewish neighborhood to live in.

SALLY

**SARITA** — Hebrew: Sarah. *Little princess.*

Sarita will have four princess phones and twelve extensions — three different telephone numbers — and a mouth that lights up in the dark. She'll call Detroit after 6 p.m. because of the bargain rates. She won't know anyone in Detroit, but she figures it's a bargain — so she'll call there anyway.

**SELENA** — Greek: Selene. *The moon.*

Selena will be the first Jewish girl to land on the moon. She will promptly take a locker there for the season.

**SELMA** — Old Norse: Anshelm. *Fair.*

Selma is a girl who has everything a Jewish boy could want ... heavy beard, deep voice, a degree from C.C.N.Y. and a father with a thriving business.


**SHARON** — Hebrew: Sharai. *A princess.*

Sharon thinks her husband is king. A typical Jewish girl who worships her husband — she places burnt offerings before him at every meal.


**SHEENA** — Irish Gaelic: Sinc. *God is gracious.*
  Sheena was Queen of the Jungle.

Your Jewish Sheena will be a head buyer in the garment center.


**SHEILA** — Irish Gaelic: Sile. *Misty-eyed.*

Sheilas are very sensitive and cry at the slightest thing. They are easily shocked. Sheila Rabinowitz cried during her honeymoon night in 1959 when her husband started getting undressed in the closet.


**SHIRLEY** — Old English: Scinleah. *From the bright meadow.*

Shirleys are usually very active in charity work. Shirley Rabinowitz, leading Jewish charity lady of Westchester. When the man from the Community Sex Drive called at her door she answered, "I already gave at the office!"


**SIBYL** — Greek: Sibylla. *A prophetess.*

If your daughter is named Sibyl, she will always be predicting — "You should live so long." So, if you want to have a long life, name her Sibyl.

**SIDNEY** — Old French: Saint-Denis. *From St. Denis, France.*

Go on — be different. Name your daughter Sidney. It may not be the most exotic name for a Jewish girl, but she'll command more respect when she enters the business world.

**SOPHIE** — Greek: Sophia. *Wisdom.*

When company visits on a Sunday, instead of cooking, Sophie will know enough to order up from the delicatessen.

**STEPHANIE** — Greek: Stephanos. *Crowned one.*

Stephanie will be the first one in her neighborhood to wear a babushka. She will also set a style trend in wigs, curlers and hair nets. Unfortunately, the only thing she won't have on her head is a bridal veil. After seeing her walking around in a babushka, who would be crazy enough to marry her?

**STORM** — Old English: Storm. *A tempest or storm.*

This girl will be a great judge of the elements. With just one glance she will look at an unmarried doctor and be able to tell "whether."

**SYLVIA** — Latin: Silva. *From the forest.*

Sylvia is from the suburbs. She is the type who insists her husband move the family to the suburbs because the kids need grass. When she gets there, the first thing she does is have the basement finished, so "the kids can play inside."

**TAMMY** — Hebrew: Tamar. *Palm tree.*

It is obvious that this girl will spend her life in the land of the palm tree — Florida. Then, when she reaches 65, she will retire north to Brooklyn for her health.

**TAMMY**

**TEMPEST** — Old French: Tempeste. *Stormy one.*

Tempest Tribowitz was going to send her husband Nat to the hospital on account of his knee. She went into his office one day and found a blonde on it.


**TERRY** — Greek: Tereos. *Shaped like the god Thor.*

Terry will have a measurement of 38-23-38 . . . on her *leg*! At her Junior Hadassah dance she will be voted Miss Zoftic.


**TESSIE** — Greek: Tessares. *Fourth child.*

Tessies are wild, wealthy, eccentric and have a great sense of humor. Tessie Tustadear of Riverdale, N.Y. . . . on her 54th birthday, shocked all her friends when she invited them to her Catered Change of Life.


**THELMA** — Greek: Thele. *A nursling; a little person still dependent upon her mother.*

Thelma will always be dependent upon her mother. She will have her mother take her across the street when she goes to school — at City College. After Thelma gets married, she will have dinner at her mother's house four nights a week. The dependency will come to an end when Thelma has her fifth child and asks her mother to baby-sit. Her mother will reply, "Go hire a sitter — I have my own life to lead."


**THERESA** — Greek: Theriso. *Reaper.*

Theresa is the slowest payer in her canasta crowd. Friends let her sit in only because they can holler at her.

**THYRA** — Greek: Thyreos. *Shield-bearer.*

Thyra will wear five-day deodorant pads to Sunday night dances at the Concourse Plaza. Her luck — on the sixth day she'll meet a fella.

**TOBY** — Hebrew: Tobhiyah. *The Lord is good.*

Toby is devoutly religious. She strictly observes the first of the Ten Commandments for Jewish Housewives: "Thou Shalt Eat Out on Sundays." Her husband will become an agnostic.

**TUESDAY** — Old English: Twiesdaeg. *Born on Tuesday.*

There has been a rash of newborn Jewish girls (also newborn Jewish girls with a rash) who have been given those cute new names like: Tuesday, Tracey, Bunny, Stacey and Veronica. These girls are almost always spoiled and unpredictable. They are usually the first ones in their neighborhoods to have wigs. They wear them to their junior high school graduations . . . then send them to camp with name-tapes sewn on.

**ULTIMA** — Latin: Ultima. *The most distant, aloof one.*

You can't touch Ultima with a ten-foot pole. With your hands she'll let you — but not with a ten-foot pole.

**VALERIE** — Old French: Valeriane. *Strong.*

At weddings, Valerie serves as anchor lady during the hora. She never realizes her own strength, and in her dancing frenzy she usually knocks over two hors d'oeuvre tables and the caterer's son. They keep inviting her anyway; Valerie gives $75.

**VANESSA** — New Latin: Vanessa. *Butterfly; a handsome woman compared to the butterfly.*

Vanessa will be beautiful but flighty. She will flit from love affair to love affair — from Murray to Harvey to Seymour — to Harriet. She will end her life like the butterfly. They will come after her with a net!

**VELVET** — Middle English: Velouette. *Velvety.*

A nice name for a Jewish girl — but can be confusing if you're in the garment business. When your girl grows up and a young man comes up to you and says, "I'm in love with your Velvet," you don't know whether he's talking about your daughter or your spring line.

**VERNA** — Latin: Verna. *Springlike; a spring nymph.*

If you take a bungalow every year, don't let Verna loose in the social hall alone — until *summer.*

**VIRGINIA** — Latin: Virginia. *Maidenly.*

It was Virginia who was the first to say, "Oy, not tonight. I have a headache." It was Jake, her husband, who was the first to say, "Call my lawyer. I'm getting a divorce."

**VIVIAN** — Latin: Viva. *Alive; lively.*

Vivian is the most active organization lady in the neighborhood. She is usually an officer of Hadassah, B'nai B'rith, United Jewish Appeal, Deborah, and also goes around collecting for Cancer Care, Boys Town, and the Fund for the Jewish Veterans of the National Football League. She is usually the first one to draw up a petition against the landlord of an apartment house. This, despite the fact that she lives in a private house three blocks away.

**WANDA** — Old German: Wanda. *Wanderer.*

Wanda Zaroff, famous escapee from a day camp in the Catskills, 1948. Was discovered years later living in self-imposed exile in a bungalow colony, near Monticello.

WANDA

**WANETTA** — Old English: Wann. *Pale one.*

Wanetta can best be described as a professional blind date. Wanetta Weinberg, Boro Park's Ugliest Girl. When she got undressed to go to bed, the fellow across the street pulled *down* his shade! When she "came on down" to Miami, Jim Dooley got so upset that he flew back up.

**YETTA** — Old English: Gaetan. *To give; giver.*

Yettas are usually older aunts — with moustaches. They are always very generous and at Bar Mitzvahs and weddings they give you a $50 bond — together with a big wet kiss.

**YVONNE** — Old French: Yves. *Yew bow.*

Yvonne Ginsberg, well-known Tel Aviv carhop. First Jewish girl to give birth to Siamese twins. She had no luck, though, as her husband immediately filed for a separation.

**ZELDA** — Old German: Grisja-hilde. *Gray battle maiden.*

Zelda is usually Yetta's daughter. She gives a smaller bond, but has a bigger moustache. She usually sits at the children's table, until she's 45.

**ZENIA** — Greek: Zenia. *Hospitable one.*

Will work in a hospital. She will be a practical nurse. The Jewish practical nurse is the one who marries a wealthy doctor.

# BOYS

**ABRAHAM** — Hebrew: Abraham. *Father of the multitude.*

Abraham will have 14 children — all girls! When the first daughter gets married, he will comfort his wife by saying, "Sarah, don't think of it as losing a daughter. Think of it as gaining a bathroom."

**ACE** — Latin: As. *Unity.*

Ace will grow up to be a pinochle player.

**ADLER** — Old German. Adlar. *Eagle.*

Name your kid Adler and he'll write a book about it someday.

**ADRIAN** — Latin: Ater. *Dark one.*

Jewish Adrians either become hairdressers — or choreographers in the Yiddish theater.

**ALAN** — Irish Gaelic: Alain. *Handsome, cheerful, harmonious one.*

With this kind of disposition Alan is bound to become a successful used-car dealer. He will specialize in selling and distributing the Jewish car — the Simcha.

**ALBERT** — Old English: Aethelberht. *Noble and brilliant or industrious.*

Albert will graduate in the upper 25 percent of his class at the NYU School of Commerce. He will pass the CPA exam on his first try. His mother will wake up all the neighbors to tell them.

**ALEXANDER** — Greek: Alexandros. *Helper and defender of mankind.*

Alexander will grow up to be a department store in New York.

**ALFRED** — Old English: Aelfraed. *Good or elfin counselor.*

Alfred will become a counselor after being a camper for 14 years. One year his mother will forget to sew name tapes on the back of his shirts. For that entire summer he will be known as "Fruit of the Loom."

**ALVIN** — Old German: Alh-win. *Friend of all; noble friend.*

At the Family Circles or Cousins Club meetings, Alvin is the guy who offers to drive everybody home. It usually turns out that he lives someplace out on Long Island — and they all live in New Jersey. This is a two-day drive from his house, without traffic.

**AMOS** — Hebrew: Amos. *A burden.*

Amos epitomizes all the Jewish men who have similar burdens. He's the guy who walked into his psychiatrist's office and said, "Doctor, I have a problem. I have a beautiful $60,000 home in Rockville Centre, a $20,000 summer home in Palm Springs, a gorgeous wife who has an $8,000 ermine coat and a $12,000 Cadillac." The doctor said, "Mr. Teitlebaum, that's wonderful. But what's your problem?" Teitlebaum said, "I only make $55 a week."

**ANDREW** — Greek: Andreas. *Strong; manly.*

Andrew is the strong, manly type. At the Seder dinner, he will be asked to open up the horse-radish, bring in the bridge chairs from the bedroom, and carry in the lazy Susan — who turns out to be his fat cousin from out of town.

**BARRY** — Irish Gaelic: Bearach. *Spearlike or pointed.*
   Barry Goldwater — Senator and Presidential candidate.

Like his contemporary political namesake, Barry will be half-Jewish. He will come to a country club for a day of golf. It will be restricted. A man will say, "Sorry, sir — we're restricted — no Jews allowed." Barry will protest, "But I'm only half-Jewish." So they let him play nine holes.

**BARTHOLOMEW** — Hebrew: Bar-Tamai. *A farmer; guardian of the plow.*

Bartholomew will be a Jewish hillbilly. Summers he will get a job as social director in the mountains — the Ozarks. He will lead the guests in a game of Simon Sayeth, and then will join them in singing some classic Jewish hillbilly folk tunes: "Schlep to My Lou," "Once There Was Greenfield," "Oh, My Darlin' Eisenstein," "Kisses Sweeter Than Borscht," "Oh, The Long Island Line," and the popular, "Jimmy Crack Cohen — and I Don't Care."

**BENJAMIN** — Hebrew: Binyamin. *Favorite son.*

Being the favorite son, Benjamin will be forced to go into his father's business — whether he likes it or not. His mother will give him arguments like: "It is so terrible his business? He didn't make a good living from it all these years? If it's good enough for him — it's good enough for *you*." So — what's his father's business? He's a wholesaler for *Colliers* magazine and the *New York Mirror*.

**BERGER** — French: Berger. *Shepherd.*

It's a strange occupation for a Jewish boy (it's a strange occupation for *any* boy). He will get his shepherd's job through the want ads of the *Daily Forward*. When people ask his folks what Berger does, they'll reply, "He's in woolens."

**BERNARD** — Old German: Nerin-hard. *Bold as a bear.*

Bernies are bold. They are born with *chutzphah.* Bernie is the type who boldly gets up to the microphone at his own Bar Mitzvah and announces: "Don't send me presents — give me *cash!*" When he gets engaged, his future father-in-law will question him. "Do you think you can support my daughter on $75 a week?" Bernard's reply, "Well, if that's the best you can do, Mr. Teitlebaum, I'll have to try."

**BORIS** — Slavic: Boris. *Battler; spirited.*
Boris Karloff — actor, horror movies.

With Boris every night it's "Shock Theater." He marries a girl named Selma who is apt to walk into the living room in curlers with a mudpack on. He doesn't know whether to kiss her or set a trap.

**BOYCHICK —**

No actual meaning — just a nice Jewish name.

**CAESAR** — Latin: Caesar. *Emperor.*
Julius Caesar, victim of a vicious plot to overthrow him from power.

History will repeat itself and there will be an attempt to overthrow him when he decides to go into business with his two brothers-in-law — on his wife's side.

**CALVERT** — Old English: Calfhierde. *Calf herder.*

Calvert is the big drinker at B'nai B'rith affairs. He will have rye after rye after rye. Finally, after eight slices he will get shika and collapse. Although he drinks a lot, Calvert will be reserved.

**CAMPBELL** — Scotch Gaelic: Cam-beul. *Wry or crooked mouth.*

This kid will cost you a fortune in orthodontic work. But he will make up for it in later years when he himself becomes a dentist. Campbell will follow in the trend of Orthodox Jewish dentists. He will change the plates every Passover.

**CAREY** — Old Welsh: Caerau. *Dweller at the castles.*

Carey will spend his entire life living in apartment houses. His philosophy will be: "Look, why should I move to a home in Long Island if I can live comfortable in an apartment house and let the super do all the work?" He will end up breaking his neck from a fall down a fire escape.

**CASEY** — Irish Gaelic: Cathasach. *Valorous.*

Casey will end up being a ballplayer or a railroad engineer. If you want a doctor or a lawyer, forget this name.

**CECIL** — Latin: Caecilius. *Dim-sighted; misty-eyed.*

Cecil is the boy who gets lost and cries at Coney Island when he runs out on the beach — and then finds he can't get back into the locker section because his hand wasn't stamped. Cecil will disappear completely at the age of 29.

**CHARLTON** — Old English: Carla-tun. *Peasant's farmstead or town.*
   Charlton Heston — actor.

Charlton will play Moses in a pageant in Hebrew school. He will forget his lines after the Third Commandment.

**CHRISTIAN** — Greek: Christos. *Anointed one.*

Will have difficulty convincing people he's Jewish. They will suspect something wrong when he goes into a delicatessen and orders a corned-beef and pastrami sandwich — "on date-nut bread."

**CLARENCE** — Latin: Clarensis. *Famous one.*

Clarence Trumbanick, famous Jewish inventor of hospital supplies. Among them: oral syringes, custom-made bedpans, four-color X-ray pictures, machine-made circumcisions and oxygen tents with Arizona air.

**COLE** — Greek: Nikolaus. *Conqueror.*
   Cole Porter — American composer.

Cole will grow up to be a great popular songwriter — writing such songs as: "Throw Mama from the Train a Knish . . . a knish," and "I kiss your arms, I kiss your lips, my hearts on fire! I kiss your arms, I kiss your lips, cause you're a buyer!"

**CYRANO** — Greek: Kurene. *From Cyrene.*
   Cyrano de Bergerac, hero of Rostand's classic drama.

Cyrano will have a very long nose. He will become a beatnik and let his hair grow very long. He will achieve fame in his neighborhood when at the age of 14 he places second in a Barbra Streisand — Look Alike Contest.

**DAGWOOD** — Old English: Daegga's wode. *Bright one's forest.*

Dagwood is the type who will make himself a tremendous sandwich of lox, cream cheese, herring, anchovies and salami — all on a bialy. Dagwood is very concerned with food. He believes a woman's place is in the stove.

**DALBERT** — Old English: Deal-beorht. *Proud, brilliant one.*

Dalbert is the proud one. He's the only fellow in the synagogue who gives a pledge without making them call his name out.

**DALE** — Old English: Dael. *Dweller in the valley.*

Will dwell in the San Fernando Valley — and become one of California's leading movie producers. Will produce such outstanding Jewish films as: *El Sid, Around the World in 80 Days — Maybe 70, Gidget Gets Bas-Mitzvahed, Mary Popkin, Larry of Arabia, Frankenstein Meets the Seltzer Man, Taras' Bubba, It's a Mishugana, Mishugana, Mishugana, Mishugana World,* and the haunting *All About Irv.*

**DANIEL** — Hebrew: Daniyel. *God is my judge.*
   Dan Dailey, Danny Thomas, Danny Kaye, Dan Duryea.

A Daniel, or Danny, usually turns out to be a social director at a summer resort. He is generally a short guy with curly hair, and is great at conducting sessions of Simon Sez. One Danny pulled the practical joke of the season when he arranged for a group of doctors and lawyers to visit the hotel and tell the girls they were shipping clerks.

**DAVID** — Hebrew: David. *Beloved one.*

David is overly loved and spoiled rotten by his family. Everytime an uncle or a zayda comes to visit David, they give him $5. He's the only kid in the neighborhood to walk around with a wallet in his diaper.

**DENNIS** — Greek: Dionys-os. *God of wine.*

Actually Dennis won't dig wine that much, but he *will* be the champion chugalugger of egg creams from the Bronx to Sheepshead Bay. When he grows up, Dennis will ride shotgun on a seltzer truck.


**DEVIN** — Irish Gaelic: Daimhin. *Poet; savant.*

Devin Rabinowitz, brilliant poet-savant. Author of widely acclaimed book, *How to Live in Bensonhurst on $5 a Day.*


**DILLON** — Irish Gaelic: Diolmhain. *Faithful one.*

Most Jewish men are faithful and are very surprised when they find a Jewish wife who isn't. Dillon Abromowitz, for example, came home one night and found his wife in the arms of his best friend. Dillon was shocked, and said, "Hymie, I must . . . but *you*?"


**DUANE** — Irish Gaelic: Dubhain. *Little dark one.*

Will try to become suntanned every summer by going up to the roof and lying on tar beach. Unfortunately, Duane will not live in an apartment house — but in a private house with a slanty roof. He will constantly find himself sliding off.


**DUKE** — Old French: Duc. *Leader.*

Duke is the leader of his neighborhood gang. He is a tough kid who slicks his hair back with chicken fat. His upper-middle-class parents give him every opportunity but he fails. At the age of five he becomes a nursery school dropout. As a teen ager he will be arrested for painting Jewish Stars of David on Volkswagens in the middle of the night.

**DURWARD** — Old English: Duru-weard. *Gatekeeper.*

A Jewish boy named Durward will someday assume the highest gate-keeping position open to a boy of his faith. He will work as an entrance guard at the Fontainebleau Hotel in Miami Beach.


**EARL** — Irish Gaelic: Airleas. *A pledge.*

Earl is usually the fellow who raises his hand and pledges $500 to the schule. He ends up giving $15, but he pledges $500.


**EDMUND** — Old English: Eadmund. *Prosperous protector.*

Will be police commissioner of a prosperous Jewish community like Tel Aviv, Jerusalem or Beverly Hills. It was Edmund Goldfarb, noted law enforcer of Tel Aviv who said, "Crime does not pay — but at least you're your own boss."


**EDSEL** — Old English: Ead-sele. *A prosperous man's manor house.*

Name your son Edsel and he'll grow up to be a loser. As a child he will learn only two of the Four Kashas. Edsel is the kind of a guy who takes out fire insurance and the very next day has a flood.


**EDWIN** — Old English: Eadwine. *Prosperous friend.*

Edwin is the boy who makes $400 a week pushing a hand truck in the garment center. His boss likes him. He's Edwin's father-in-law.


**ELI** — Hebrew: Eli. *The highest.*

Eli always lives on the *top* floor of a 10-story, luxury apartment house in Forest Hills. Eli thinks the novel *From the Terrace* is the life story of a Long Island builder.

EDWIN

**ELMER** — Old English: Aethelmaere. *Of awe-inspiring fame.*

Elmer Epstein worked in the research department of a Fairfax Avenue catering hall. He became world famous when he invented what is now a must item at all weddings and Bar Mitzvahs — chopped liver in the shape of a swan.

**ELVIS** — Old Norse: Alviss. *All wise.*

Elvis will become a popular rock-and-roll singer. He will be the first person in the history of the synagogue to lip-synch his Bar Mitzvah speech to a previously taped record.

**EMIL** — Latin: Aemilius. *Optimistic one.*

Emil is the typical young newlywed who says to his wife, "Look, while you're working and until we have a child, we'll live on my salary and save yours." Not only do they end up living on her salary also, but he has to get a second job nights. They both would starve if his mother didn't bring them food every Thursday.

**ERIC** — Old Norse: Ei-rik-r. *Ever powerful; ever ruler.*

Eric will turn out to be the powerful local mobster and gambler in the neighborhood. He will openly flaunt the law. He will use a bookie joint as a front for a candy store.

**EUGENE** — Greek: Eugenios. *Well-born; noble.*

Eugene is usually born in a fashionable Jewish section like Bronxville. Despite his religion, he attends Choate, Princeton and the N.Y.A.C. He surprises everybody by marrying a nice Jewish girl. He's the type that joins a "very" Reformed temple. It's usually called "Our Lady of a Thousand Mitzvahs."

**EZRA** — Hebrew: Ezra. *Help; helper.*

Ezra will become a doctor, specializing in "recommending." He won't treat anybody. He'll just recommend you to another doctor.

**FARFEL** — Yiddish: Far-fallen. *Too late.*

Farfel is the cute little boy whom everyone loves, but he never learns to speak correctly. He says things like, "Hey, Ma, throw me down the stairs a quarter." Also, "Up the street, the soldiers are coming down." When he grows up, he will get a job as an interpreter at the U.N.

**FARRELL** — Irish Gaelic: Fearghal. *Most valorous one.*

Farrell is the strong and powerful type. He can lift the Sunday paper with one hand. At 35 he will get a hernia and open a truss shop on Sixth Avenue.

**FELIX** — Latin: Felix. *Fortunate, lucky one.*

Felix is the world's luckiest Jew. He has a wife and a color TV set — and they both work!

**EZRA**

**FERRIS** — Irish Gaelic: Feoras. *Very choice one.*

Name the kid Ferris and he's got to become a big wheel.


**FILBERT** — Old English: Felabeorhit. *Very brilliant one.*

Filbert Kleinman, brilliant Jewish medical researcher. Once discovered a cure for which there was no known disease. Gave up after trying to get the 7-year itch marked down to 5½.


**FLINT** — Old English: Flint. *A stream.*

Make sure you hire a diaper service for this kid. It was Flint Rabinowitz who in the first grade walked up to his teacher and said, "I gotta go." The teacher said, "When you have to go, raise two fingers." Flint said, "OK, but I don't think that will help."


**FRANCIS** — Latin: Franciscus. *Free man — a man who thinks for himself.*

Three scientists, a Frenchman, a German and a Jew (Francis) were told by a doctor they had only one month to live. Therefore, they could have any last request. The Frenchman said, "I want wine, women and song." The German said, "I want to go back to the beer halls of Vienna and sing." Francis Nussbaum said, "To tell you the truth, I'd like to see another doctor."


**FRANKLIN** — Middle English: Frankeleyn. *Free holder of land.*
A man who earned his freedom from his overlord.

Frank is the kind of guy who never has trouble breaking his apartment house lease and getting back his deposit. The reason: the first thing all Franks do when they move in is shmear the renting agent and take care of the super.

**FLINT**

**FREDERICK** — Old German: Fridu-rik. *Peaceful ruler.*

Fredericks are usually so peaceful that they're *henpecked.* Frederick Fishkind of New Rochelle was so henpecked that he didn't complain when his wife took the car to play Mah-Jongg — seven nights in a row — *during their honeymoon.*

**FRICK** — Old English: Freca. *Bold man.*

Frick will be a "bold" businessman. He will be the first merchant in his neighborhood to have a Pre-Fire Sale.

**GARY** — Old English: Gari. *Spear; spearman.*

Gary Baumgarten, first man to carry a pointed spear in an Israeli operatic production. He was fired his first day for accidentally bumping into the coloratura. He did, however, bring about the highest note she ever sang.

**GAYLORD** — Old French: Gaillord. *Lively one.*
 Gaylord Ravenal — Famous *Showboat* Mississippi gambler.

Gaylord Rabinowitz, first gambler on a Mississippi riverboat ever to attempt a game of pinochle. Later turned to a life of crime. He started holding up Chinese restaurants. He would go in, whip out a gun, and say, "Give me all your money — to take out!"

**GEARY** — Middle English: Gery. *Changeable one.*

Could never make up his mind. At the age of six when they asked him, "What do you want to be when you grow up?" he replied, "An accountant." Then at 31, he changed his mind and decided to become a cowboy.

**GERARD** — Old English: Garhard. *Prosperous spearman.*

Gerard will grow up to become a very successful mohel.

GARY

**GERONIMO** — (Form of Jerome) — Latin: Hieronymus. *Sacred or holy name.*

Geronimo is the name you give to a Jewish Indian. He will encounter much prejudice. When he grows up he will find that many people are anti-Seminole.

**GODFREY** — Old German: Gott-fried. *Divinely peaceful.*
Arthur Godfrey — TV personality.

Godfrey Meyerwitz. Israel's biggest TV star. (For many years he was known as "Mr. Erev Tuesday Night".) He was famed for taking popular American entertainment and adapting it into Hebrew. He did a weekly musical variety segment called, "That Wonderful Year — 5721." He also composed a sentimental love ballad called, "Will You Love Me in the Month Of Kislev-Teveth As You Do in Sivan?" Godfrey's greatest success was when he brought over the TV series "Run For Your Life" . . . the story of an Arab on Delancey Street.

**GOWER** — Old Welsh: Gwyr. *Pure one.*

Gower is the kid everybody takes advantage of. At Gower's divorce, his wife will get custody of any kids he has by his next wife.


**GREGORY** — Latin: Gregorius. *Watchman; watchful one.*

Gregory usually sits on his terrace and watches what everyone else in the apartment house is doing. He sometimes marries a girl named Abby. Together, they are the scourge of the neighborhood.


**GUY** — Old German: Wide. *Warrior.*

Lives dangerously. At a Bensonhurst dance, he found a girl he liked and took her home to meet his family — his wife and three kids.


**HALL** — Old English: Heale. *Dweller at the hall.*

Hall lives up to his name. When company comes, he's the one who will sleep in the foyer.


**HARDY** — Old German: Harti. *Bold and daring.*

Hardy is so bold and daring that we're afraid to do a joke about his name.


**HAROLD** — Old Norse: Harvald. *Army leader.*

Harold came from a very kosher home — and thus was court-martialed in 1962 when he refused to attack the Bay of Pigs.

**HAROLD**

**HARRY** — Old English: Hari. *Army man.*
Harry Truman, President of the U.S.

After Harry leaves the Army he usually becomes a haberdasher. On Sundays he pals around with Sol. They go to a candy store for an egg cream. Then they go to Sol's house and watch the Giant's football game. Harry always has a bet on the game. Sol always falls asleep. They have nothing in common. They are good friends.

**HARTMAN** — Old German: Hart-mann. *Strong, austere man.*

Hartman "Hesh" Hartman, a strong, but very vain garment center shipping clerk. For his two-week summer vacation in the mountains, Hartman bought a toupee — and kept it on with thumbtacks.

**HARVEY** — Old Breton French: Huerv. *Bitter; severe.*
Harvey Firestone — American industrialist.

Harvey Fishbein — great Jewish-American industrialist of the twentieth century. Working in the research department of a giant soap company, he invented the first Jewish detergent — Vel.

**HENRY** — Old German: Heimrik. *Ruler of an estate, a home, or private property.*

Henry is usually born in poverty on the Lower East Side. He will work long and hard and will eventually, one day, have his own summer home. It will be on the corner of Orchard and Delancey Streets.

**HERBERT** — Old German: Geriberaht. *Army — brilliant.*

Herbert Hershkowitz, brilliant Israeli scholar, one day went to the Jerusalem Induction Center with a note from his mother saying, "Please excuse my boy from the Army as he has a very bad cold!"

**HILARY** — Latin: Hilarius. *Cheerful, gay one.*

Try to ignore the cheerful and gay spirit of Hilary; he'll outgrow it. Start worrying, however, if during his wedding ceremony, he ignores the bride — and starts kissing the rabbi.

**HIRAM** — Hebrew: Hiram. *Most noble one.*

It was Hiram Hershkowitz who said (while discussing his fiancée — Estelle), "A woman should be placed under a pedestal."

**HOWARD** — Old English: Heah-weard. *Chief guardian.*

Howard is the type who, whenever he goes to the beach, an old lady comes over to him and says, "Mister, you'll watch my blanket?"

**HUDSON** — Old English: Hodsane. *Son of the hooded one.*

Hudson Birnbaum, noted organization man. He couldn't help it, but Hudson was brought up in rural South Carolina where his father was a member of the Ku Klux Klan. Hudson broke away, however, and came north to marry a nice Jewish girl from Bensonhurst. He soon found himself to be the Imperial Wizard of the B'nai B'rith.

**HYMAN** — Hebrew: Hhayim. *Long life.*

Hymie will have a long and healthy life. Retaining his potency and sexual vigor for a very long time, Hymie is the guy that gets married at 90 to a 22-year-old girl — because he *has* to.

**IAN** — Scotch Gaelic: Laian. *God is gracious.*

Ian is a nice Orthodox Jewish boy. He will be expelled from public school however. They will catch him praying in the back of the classroom.

**IGNATIUS** — Latin: Ignatius. *Fiery or ardent one.*

When war comes, Ignatius is the first Jewish boy in the neighborhood to rush down to his draft board and volunteer. They will turn him down, telling him they have enough boys working on the draft board.

**IRA** — Hebrew: Ira. *Watchful one.*

Ira is the kind of a guy who, when he goes into a store to order a half pound of lox, makes sure he gets exactly a half pound of lox. While he is watching the scale, however, somebody walks off with his bagels.

**HYMAN**

**IRVING** — Old English: Earwine. *Sea friend.*

It pays to go to the beach with a fella named Irving. His mother always packs an extra sandwich which he is always offering you. It's usually a chicken salad on onion roll. You will love the sandwich but hate Irving.

**IRWIN** — Old English: Earwine. *Sea friend.*

Irwin hates Irving.*

**ISAAC** — Hebrew: Yitshbag. *He laugheth.*
Isaac was sacrificed on the altar by his father, Abraham.

Isaac will display a sense of humor while he is being sacrificed on the altar — during his wedding. Recently, in the middle of a marriage ceremony, an Isaac was asked by the rabbi, "Do you promise to love, honor and obey?" Isaac retorted, "Would you believe two out of three?"

**ISADORE** — Greek: Isidoros. *Gift of Isis.*

Isadore is a world traveler. He went to the bullfights in Mexico. At the gate he watched the bullfighters enter. The first one walked in and told the guard, "Toreador!" The guard said, "Sí. Entre." The next one said, "Picador!" The guard said, "Sí. Entre." Then Isadore thought he'd try it. He boldly walked up and shouted, "Isadore!" The guard nodded and said, "Shalom, Kimt aran!" (Hello. Come on in.)

**JACOB** — Hebrew: Ya'agob. *The supplanter or reaper.*

Jacob usually winds up as the doctor at Mt. Sinai Hospital who is always called in when they want another medical opinion. He invariably agrees with the other doctors so that's why they keep him around.

---

*But he likes Ira.

**JEFFREY** — Old French: Geoffroi. *Divinely peaceful.*

Jeffreys have always been contented, peaceful little boys. As the story goes, Jeffrey Feinstein was being wheeled along West End Avenue by his nurse, when along came Mrs. Zimmerman. She said hello to the nurse then asked, "So this is little Jeffrey, how old is he now?" The nurse said, "Nine years old." Mrs. Zimmerman was shocked and gasped, "Nine years old — and still in a carriage?" Jeffrey then stuck his head out and shouted, "Mrs., I'm bothering you?"

**JEROME** — Latin: Hieronymus. *Sacred or holy name.*

Jerome is always the guy who gets stuck being an usher at friends' weddings. At the end of the year he has 17 tiepins, 41 sets of cuff links (that don't match), 3 monogrammed money clips (with the wrong monogram) and a bill for $600 in tuxedo rentals. By the way, Jerome himself never gets married.


**JESSE** — Hebrew: Yishay. *Wealth.*
   Jesse James — noted outlaw.

Jesse Jacobson — wealthy Jewish outlaw. He was the one who held up the Yiddish stage — on Second Avenue. He got away with $14, the prompter, two old ladies from the mezzanine, and 12 pounds of halvah from the candy counter.


**JONAS** — Hebrew: Yonah. *Dove; peace-loving.*
   Jonas Salk — noted physician and researcher — the Salk vaccine.

It was a Jonas who also gave us the definition of chicken soup — "Jewish penicillin."


**JONATHAN** — Hebrew: Y-honathan. *Jehovah's gift.*

Jonathan usually considers himself God's gift to women. He invariably goes up to the mountains every summer. He's usually a shipping clerk, but for those two weeks he tells everybody he's a lawyer. He then uses lines like, "Didn't I meet you at an over-28 club dance in the city?" — "Who needs it, it's just a rat race!" And the popular, "Please be gentle. It's my first time."


**JORDAN** — Hebrew: Yarden. *Descender.*

Jordan is completely without feelings or emotion. He will fail the Rorschach Test by turning in a blank paper.

**90**

**JOSEPH** — Hebrew: Yoseph. *He shall add.*

Joseph will be the first one on his block to be a CPA. His mother will have a lot of *naches* (happiness) from him. Accounting will be his whole life. When he meets girls he will hit them with his stock line: "Darling, each minute away from you is like 60 seconds."

**JULIUS** — Latin: Julius. *Youthful, downy-bearded one.*

Julius will either become a beatnik attending NYU — or a rabbinical student at Yeshiva University.

**KARL** — Old German: Karl. *Strong; manly.*

Karl is a "schtarkah," a "bull van." He's the strongest guy around — but he's got one problem — he's a hypochondriac. As a teenager he goes to drive-in movies in an ambulance. Karl lives to be 90. On his grave he has written the epitaph: "See — I told you I was sick!"

**KEITH** — Irish Gaelic: Caith. *From the battle place.*

Keith will be a news commentator for a Jewish radio station — who will cover the action live from the "battle fronts of the world." He will open each broadcast with these words: "Good evening. What kind of a day has it been? Don't ask!"

**KENNETH** — Irish Gaelic: Coinneach. *Handsome one.*

Kenneth is usually a swinger. Every weekend he goes up to a hotel in South Fallsburg and gives the girls ultimatums. He says things like, "I'm only here till Sunday." They invariably answer, "I'm dancing as fast as I can!" Kenneth will not make out until he gets married.

**KIRK** — Old Norse: Kirkja. *Dweller at the church.*

Kirk will dwell at the synagogue. He will be extremely Orthodox. As a baby he will amaze his parents with his first words: רושיע.

באַאמטע האָבן מורא, אַז די צאָל
קרבנות וועט זיין אַ סך גרעסער.
נאָך סטעיט טרופּערס זענען

JULIUS

**KYLE** — Irish Gaelic: Caol. *From the strait.*

A Kyle may wind up in a straitjacket. He is apt to be a little absent-minded. Kyle Kirshenbaum, after his wedding, got a bit confused. He gave his wife cuff links — and went off on his honeymoon with one of the ushers.

**LANG** — Old Norse: Lang-r. *Long or tall man.*

Lang will be the outstanding basketball player at his Yeshiva. He will proudly walk around campus with the school letters on his sweater: "Gimmel" and "Dallid." He will be called — "Langah — Luksh."

**LEO** — Latin: Leo. *Lion.*

Leo is usually the guy who came over from Europe as an immigrant in the early 1900's. He will claim he arrived with only one dollar in his pocket. This is true — but he had $40,000 sewn in the lining.

**LEON** — French: Leon. *Lionlike.*
   Leon Uris — author of *Exodus.*

Leon Vrowitz, noted Jewish author. Wrote *Son of Exodus*, a story of the movement of Jewish people — from Boro Park to Great Neck. The book never sold. Leon still lives in Brooklyn.

**LEONARD** — Old Frankish: Leon-hard. *Lion-brave.*
   Leonard Bernstein, composer – conductor, musician.

Leonard will have natural rhythm. After his Bar Mitzvah song, the guests in the congregation will be so carried away by his rhythm, they will shout up to him, ecstatically, "One more time!"

**LANG**

**LINDY** — From Lindberg, Old German: Linde-berg. *Linden Tree Hill.*

Name your son Lindy and he's bound to turn up in the restaurant and catering business. If, at the age of 16, as a waiter in the mountains — he serves soup with a shaky hand — he shows potential for becoming one of the great Jewish waiters of all time. He's got it made, if at home, his mother asks him, "Lindy, tzatskaleh — you'll get me a glass tea." He says, "Sorry, this isn't my section."

**LOUIS** — Old German: Hlutwig. *Famous warrior.*

Louis is always arguing with his wife. At their wedding in the Flatbush Jewish Center, he will say, "I do." She will say, "I do." This will be the last time they'll ever agree.

**MANNY** — German: Mandel. *Almond.*

Manny will be a sweet guy — but kind of a nebbish. Things will always be happening to *him*. Manny will be the only person of the Jewish faith ever to go up to Darien, Connecticut . . . and be thrown out of a restricted miniature golf course.

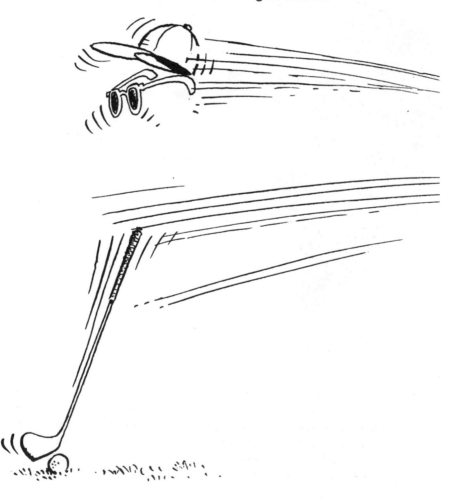

**MARK** — Latin: Marcus. *Warlike one.*

Mark is warlike and likes to live dangerously. He plays Russian roulette with six cartridges, drives an open-top Volkswagen down Flatbush Avenue, and while working for a travel agency, he arranges for an Arab to spend two weeks at Grossinger's at the height of the season.

**MARLON** — Old French: Esmerillon. *Little falcon or hawk.*

Marlon Brandenburg, itinerant Jewish hawker of religious gimmicks. Among them, mezuzahs for charm bracelets, skullcaps that glow in the dark and removable beards for old Jewish ladies who want to sit with the men in synagogues.

**MARTIN** — Latin: Martinus. *Warlike one.*

Martin usually loves the Army. One of them wrote to his mother, "Dear Mom: The battle is terrible. I'm right here in the middle of the fighting and in a minute I'll be in the thick of hand-to-hand combat." She wrote back: "Dear Marty: Don't butt in."

**MAURICE** — Late Latin: Mauricius. *Dark-complexioned one.*

Maurice is really Morris after his parents move to the suburbs. See Morris. (For Morris see Mendel.) (For Mendel see Moishe.) (For Moishe see your doctor.)

**MELVIN** — Old English: Maelwine. *Sword friend or speech friend.*

Melvin is usually a schlemiel. In the restaurant the waiter spills soup on Melvin's jacket. When we get to the head of the line we find it's *his* car that's stalled. And when he tries breaking up a street fight it's *his* body we find in the alley. Melvin Umglick, the first Jewish fellow in his neighborhood to buy an Edsel.

**MENDEL** — East Semitic: Min'da. *Knowledge; wisdom.*

With his knowledge and wisdom he'll soon change his name anyway — so forget it!


**MILES** — Late Latin: Miles. *Soldier; warrior.*

Miles Teitlebaum, Jewish soldier and hero. Invented the Karate blow in 1546 B.C. Planned to use it against the Philistines, but never got a chance. Two days before the battle, he accidentally killed himself while saluting.


**MONTGOMERY** — Old French: Mont-Gomeric. *From the wealthy one's hill.*

Montgomery will come from a wealthy hill (Beverly Hills or Forest Hills), but he himself will be poor. He will save whatever he can but will be ashamed of his economic position. When he gets married, he will tell his wife, "Honey, I'm sorry, but for our honeymoon I can only afford to take you to Florida." "What's so wrong with honeymooning in Florida?" "The Everglades?"


**MOSES** — Hebrew: Mosheh. *Taken out of water.*

Moses swims like a fish, climbs high mountains, leads long hikes — then comes home for Passover and finds there's no bread in the house.


**MURRAY** — Scotch Gaelic: Morogh. *Mariner; sea warrior.*

Murrays are always the guys who go on ocean cruises with their wives. It's unfortunate because most Jewish Murrays aren't cut out for an ocean voyage. Many Murrays have gotten seasick just looking at a shipping clerk. The one famous nautical Murray of the high seas was Captain Murray Ahab, who in the nineteenth century spent his entire life trying to capture the great white herring who bit off his leg. The name of the herring — Moby Shtick.

**MONTGOMERY**

**NATHAN** — Hebrew: Nathan. *A gift or given of God.*

Nathans usually have a gift of philosophy and insight. It was Nathan Shlefferman, on the sixth day of his honeymoon who philosophized, "Marriage is like a warm bath. Once you get used to it, it's not so hot."

**NEAL** — Irish Gaelic: Niall. *Champion.*

Neal is a champion of his people. An adventurous spirit, he is not afraid to face new challenges and overcome all obstacles. Neal is the first in his crowd to get a nose job.

**NELSON** — English: Neil-son. *Champion's son.*

With a son like Nelson, you'll be saying at least one of the following every day: "You're making me gray before my time." "I sacrifice day and night and this is what I get?" "A nervous wreck you're making out of me!" "Believe me, I'm only doing it for your own good!" and the classic, " Wait until your father comes home!"

**NORMAN** — Old French: Normand. *A Northman.*

Norman is the original hard-luck kid. He gets to the box office a second after the prices change. He washes his car a minute before it starts to rain. Norman still buys things retail.

**OGDEN** — Old English: Okedene. *From the oak valley.*

Name the kid Ogden only if you happen to live in Utah. But whichever way you look at it — funny, it doesn't sound Jewish!

**OSWALD** — Old English: Osweald. *Divinely powerful.*

Oswald Nussbaum, powerful Yiddish copywriter. Creator of the slogan: "You Don't Have to Be Levy to Enjoy Jewish Bread!"

**OTTO** — Old German: Otto. *Prosperous, wealthy one.*

Otto is so wealthy he had his gallstones removed — and rhinestones put in.

**PATRICK** — Latin: Patricius. *Noble one.*

Patrick Rosensweig, noble Yiddish humanitarian. Introduced the first Foul-Air Fund in upstate New York. His slogan, "Help Send Country Boys to the City!"

**PAUL** — Latin: Paulus. *Little.*

Paul will be little and frail, but will have a sense of humor. There was the story of Paul Zimmelzetz — a heavy smoker. His doctor told him he had a choice between cigarettes and cancer — so he gave up cancer.

PAUL

**PHILIP** — Greek: Philippas. *Lover of horses.*

Philip spends his evenings at Yonkers Raceway, N.Y., his afternoons at Aqueduct, N.Y., and his mornings betting on the merry-go-round at Palisades Park, N.J. This put a terrible strain on his wife — because they all live in Beverly Hills, Calif. Philip is the guy who takes his wife to the track and along about the seventh race says, "Remember the money I told you not to give me under *any* circumstances." She says, "Yes." He says, "I'm ready for it now."

**QUENTIN** — Latin: Quinctus. *Fifth child.*

Impossible! Today Jewish parents just aren't having five children. Either name him something else — or check your rhythm.

**RANDOLPH** — Old English: Rand-wulf. *Shield-wolf.*

Randolph Moskowitz, first Jewish man to be bitten by a werewolf. Accused of being a Wolfman, he retreated to his castle in Transylvania (4½ rooms with terrace — 180 rubles a month) and, in his lab, proceeded to create a monster 15 feet tall with a yarmulke — he created a Finklestein.

**RAYMOND** — Old German: Ragin-mund. *Mighty or wise protector.*

Raymond Nussbaum, mighty and wise Jewish philosopher. When asked why it was that some Jewish people answer a question by asking one, he answered: "Why not?"

**REUBEN** — Hebrew: R'ubhen. *Behold a son.*

Reuben is a man who will have nothing but aggravation and tsouris from his son. Just last week, a Reuben we know, a partner in a large and prosperous Seventh Avenue clothing firm, was complaining to his friend Natie — about his offspring. "Oy, Natie," he sighed. "I don't know what I'm going to do about my son, Norman. Ever since I took him into the business — all he wants to do is pinch the models." Natie calmed him. "You're overly concerned, Reuben. It's natural — lots of young men like to pinch the models." Reuben lamented, "But, Natie — I'm in the *men's* clothing business!"

RANDOLPH

**RICHARD** — Old German: Richart. *Powerful ruler.*
Richard Tucker — opera star.

Richard will have a powerful singing voice. Richard Tuckowsky, south Brooklyn's greatest singer. Had such a powerful voice he was the first man ever to get an answer from Chloe.

**RIPLEY** — Old English: Hrypanleah. *Dweller at the shouter's meadow.*

You name him this and they'll never believe it!

**ROBERT** — Old English: Hrothbeorht. *Bright or shining with fame.*

At the B'nai B'rith convention in Washington, Robert achieved fame when President Johnson once took him aside — and left him there.

**ROGER** — Old German: Ruoder. *Famous spearman.*

Roger will become a well known *mohel* as did Roger Hymie Trubowitz who had a small store on Rivington Street. In the window of this store he had a fantastic display of watches . . . all kinds, all shapes. One day a man came into the store and said, "I'd like to buy a wristwatch." Roger said, "Sorry, I don't sell watches. I'm a mohel — I perform circumcisions." The man pointed to the window and said, "But then why do you have watches in the window?" Roger shrugged. "What *else* am I going to put there?"

**ROMEO** — Italian: Romeo. *Pilgrim to Rome.*

Romeo will give you nothing but aggravation. He'll grow a beard, move to the Village and contact you only when he needs money. Take this advice — change his name now. Make it Arnold and you're guaranteed to have a lot of *naches* (happiness).

**RONALD** — Old Norse: Rognuald. *Mighty power.*

Ronald is a fellow with guts. He will one day open up a kosher restaurant in Cairo.

**ROY** — French: Roi. *King.*

With Roy there's no in between. He either winds up being a judge or goes to the chair. For parents who like to play long shots, here's your baby.

**SAMUEL** — Hebrew: Shemuel. *His name is God.*

Samuel is the type of a son who, when he's out of town, always writes his mother once a week — even if it's only for a couple of dollars.

**SAUL** — Hebrew: Sha'ul. *Asked for.*

Saul is the type of fella that's always asking for trouble. He has a lot of courage and plenty of *chutzphah*. It was a Saul, a dapper little man from New York, who had the nerve to fly down to rural South Carolina one night and barge into the middle of a gigantic Ku Klux Klan rally. There he was . . . one little Northerner in a continental suit, standing in the midst of 3,000 hooded Southerners . . . who of course stopped what they were doing to stare at the stranger. Saul walked up to one of them and stated, "I want you should tell your leader that Saul Weingarten of Weingarten, Abromowitz and Schwartzberg is here to see him." A tall, gaunt man came over and said, "I'm Grand Dragon here. And before you go any further, Mister, let me warn ya . . . around here we hate Jews!" Saul looked up and said, "Hate — shmate . . . it doesn't bother me." The Grand Dragon was confused. "What do you want here?" Saul inquired, "Tell me, who sells you your sheets?"

**SCOTT** — Old English: Scottas. *From Scotland.*

Is of Scottish-Jewish parents. Had a wallet with pictures of his wife and mother in it — and when he lost it, he placed the following ad in the paper. "Whoever finds the wallet can keep the pictures. But for sentimental reasons, please return the money."

SAUL

**SHELDON** — Old English: Scelfdun. *From the ledge hill.*

Sheldon is the fellow you always see standing up on the hill — meditating. It was a Sheldon who came up with the definition of "mixed emotion" — "Your mother-in-law going over a cliff in your new Cadillac."

**SHERMAN** — Old English: Sceran-man. *Wool cutter.*

Sherman is the son who winds up working as a wool cutter in the garment center in order to support the other son in the family who's going to medical school. A must for all Jewish mothers who want to have a son a doctor.

**SIDNEY** — Old English: Sydney. *From St. Denis.*

Sidney is a fellow who is a big worrier. Throughout his life he is constantly aggravated and *farmisht.* At the age of four he has high blood pressure. At the age of seven he is the only one in his school with an ulcerette.

**SIMON** — Hebrew: Shim'on. *Hearing; one who hears.*

Simon will be a reporter and gossip columnist for the *Jewish Daily Forward.* Whenever he gets a scoop or a headline, he will rush excitedly into the pressroom and shout, "Hold the *back* page!"

**SOLOMON** — Hebrew: Shelomon. *Peaceful.*
   Solomon — King of Israel famous for his wisdom.

Solomons are always making wise business decisions. It was a Solomon who one day decided to get out of the wholesale fur business after 25 years. He broke the news to his partner, "Hymie, I'm quitting the fur business. I've decided instead to open a bank." Hymie was shocked. He said, "Open a bank — that's crazy. You can't just pick yourself up and go into the banking business. Besides — what are you going to call the bank?" Solomon said, "What else. I'm going to call it The Sol Trust Company." Hymie said, "What kind of a name for a bank is that — The Sol Trust Company?" Solomon said, "What — *Irving* did so bad with his!"

**STERLING** — Middle English: Sterling. *From an old English coin.*

Don't give your son this name if your last name is Silver.

**STILLMAN** — Old English: Stille-man. *Quiet man.*

Stillman Eisenberg, Israel's quietest man. His wife collected life insurance on him three times.

**TAB** — Old German: Tabbert. *Brilliant among the people.*

Tab usually turns out to be the brilliant athlete. It was Tab Teitlebaum playing on the Brooklyn College backfield in the big game against Notre Dame who had the brilliant idea to call the signals in Yiddish — so that the opposition wouldn't understand. There followed four unsuccessful plays, which were diagnosed perfectly by Notre Dame. Tab couldn't understand it — but he decided to try one last play. He bent down behind the center and yelled, *"Ain-Tsve-Drei-Fier* . . . Just then a little guy on the Notre Dame line looked up and said — *"Se vet dier goornit helfen!"* (Buddy, it's not gonna help you.)

**THEODORE** — Greek: Theodorus. *Gift of God.*

Theodore Pincus, celebrated Hebrew scientist. Famous for creating a combination caffein-benzedrine pill. You don't sleep nights but you're happy about it. In his spare time Theodore also invented a mezuzah that kisses back.

**THOMAS** — Greek: Thomas. *A twin.*

Thomas and Bernard Tannenbaum, identical Siamese twins — were the Jewish version of the Corsican Brothers. Whenever Thomas ate a hot knish — it would be Bernard who got heartburn. Then, later on in life, when Bernard opened a business — the creditors ran after Thomas.

**TIFFANY** — Old French: Tiphanie. *Divine showing; appearance of God.*

There's nothing interesting about this one other than it's a great name to sew on camp name tags.

**TREVOR** — Irish Gaelic: Treabhar. *Prudent; discreet; wise.*

Trevor Lapidus, internationally known Jewish statesman. First one wisely to note that the U.N. spelled backwards is NU?

**TYLER** — Middle English: Tylere. *Tile maker and roofer.*

Tyler Mandelbaum, world-renowned tile maker and roofer who died in 1948. As a hobby, Tyler took up the violin. In his spare time he soon began to fiddle on the roof. Then he got the brilliant idea to write a musical comedy about it. He called his play, *Mandelbaum on the Roof.* Tyler died penniless.

**URIAH** — Hebrew: Uriyah. *Flame of Jehovah.*

Uriah is the stay-at-home kind. One day you will come into your Long Island living room and find him in front of a roaring fire. This will make you very angry since you haven't got a fireplace.

**VAN** — Dutch: Van. *From or of.*

Van will run away from home at the age of 14. Let him.

TYLER

URIAH

**VERNON** — Latin: Vernum. *Springlike; youthful.*

Vernon is the guy who goes up to a hotel in the Poconos. He has a hearty lunch, goes out on the porch, sits on a rocker, breathes in the fresh air, sighs, and says, "Takke, I'll tell you the truth, I feel five years younger." Vernon is 12 years old.

**VICTOR** — Latin: Victor. *Conqueror.*

Victor tries to make it with every girl he meets. On his wedding night he had affairs with two out-of-town cousins (from his wife's side), plus a tryst with the organ lady who played "Oh Promise Me." Finally, after two years — his mother-in-law broke up his marriage. His wife came home and found him in bed with her.

**VINCENT** — Latin: Vincentius. *Conquering one.*

Vincent is usually the child of a mixed marriage. Consequently, he walks around very confused. At Christmastime he has both a Christmas tree and a Hanukkah bush. At Easter, he looks for the Easter Egg — and finds it in a box of matzos. Naturally, it's egg matzos.

**WADE** — Old English: Wace. *The advancer.*

Wade is always asking you to advance him money until payday. You ask him when payday is and he says, "How should *I* know. *You're* the one with the job!"

**WALDEN** — Old English: Wealdene. *From the forest valley.*

Walden Peckler, renowned Yiddish resort hotel operator. Famous for defining the Catskills as "a place where people go to who have already made up their minds they're having a good time."

**WALKER** — Middle English: Walkere. *Thickener of cloth.*

Walker will be in the textile business with a partner who steals from the company. The partner will also steal Walker's wife, home and children. Walker will overlook this because he can't find another partner who can cut velvet.

**WALTER** — Old German: Walthari. *Powerful leader; ruler.*

Walter is a ruler until he gets married. When you ask a henpecked Jewish husband like Walter what he did before he got married, he invariably says, "Anything I wanted to." Walter once didn't talk to his wife for three days — he didn't want to interrupt her.

**WARD** — Old English: Weard. *Watchman; guardian.*

Ward will be a lifeguard at a mikvah.

**WARNER** — Old German: Waren-hari. *Defending army or warrior.*

Warner Friedkin, famous Palestinian soldier, World War I. Fought with the boys of the 26th Infantry, 37th Infantry and 49th Infantry. He couldn't get along with anybody.

**WOODROW** — Old English: Wudo-roew. *Dweller at the hedge by the forest.*
    Woody Allen, comedian and comedy writer.

Your Woody will have a brilliant comedy mind. Woody Lifshitz, famous Haifa wit, was the creator of classic Jewish punch lines, among them: "Luke's warm to me." "When I finish this soup will you hear a scream," and the classic, "My mother — I thought she was *your* mother!" While in Tel Aviv he attempted to sell residents trees to be planted in their name in Brooklyn.

**YALE** — Old English: Healh. *From the slope or corner land.*

Yale Rubinstein, famous Ivy league medical student. He discovered that the best way to handle a heart murmur is to keep it quiet.

**YEOMAN** — Middle English: Yoman. *Retainer.*

If you think Yeoman will become a lawyer, you got a good case. But Yeomans are usually too meek to become really successful lawyers. Yeoman Yablowitz, C.C.N.Y. Law School, 1958. Was the only lawyer in history to have an ambulance chase *him.*

**ZIV** — Old Slavic: Sivu. *Living one.*

Ziv is a very lively one. He really is the end. Mainly, he's the last one on the name list. He should live and be well!